LOCAL ACTION

A CITIZEN'S GUIDE

I0884203

Published in the United States of America by Cherry Lake Publishing
Ann Arbor, Michigan
www.cherrylakepublishing.com

Content Adviser: Austin McCoy, Doctoral Candidate in History at the University of Michigan
Reading Adviser: Marla Conn MS, Ed., Literacy specialist, Read-Ability, Inc.

Photo Credits: © hxdbzxy/Shutterstock, cover, 1; © Orhan Cam/Shutterstock, 5; © MarKord/Shutterstock, 6; © Andrey Bayda/Shutterstock, 7; © Paul Vasarhelyi/Shutterstock, 8; © l i g h t p o e t/Shutterstock, 11; © DW labs Incorporated/Shutterstock, 12; © John Kershner/Shutterstock, 14; © Rawpixel.com/Shutterstock, 17; © Monkey Business Images/Shutterstock, 18, 19; © Joseph Sohm/Shutterstock, 20; © ambrozinio/Shutterstock, 23; © MaxyM/Shutterstock, 24; © Matej Kastelic/Shutterstock, 25; © Pressmaster/Shutterstock, 26; © Dmitry Morgan/Shutterstock, 28

Copyright ©2017 by Cherry Lake Publishing
All rights reserved. No part of this book may be reproduced or utilized in any form or by any means without written permission from the publisher.

Library of Congress Cataloging-in-Publication Data
Names: Mara, Wil, author.
Title: Local action / Wil Mara.
Description: Ann Arbor, Michigan : Cherry Lake Publishing, 2017. | Includes bibliographical references and index.
Identifiers: LCCN 2016003907| ISBN 9781634710701 (hardcover) | ISBN 9781634711692 (pdf) | ISBN 9781634712682 (pbk.) | ISBN 9781634713672 (ebook)
Subjects: LCSH: Local government—United States—Juvenile literature.
Classification: LCC JS331 .M277 2017 | DDC 320.80973—dc23
LC record available at http://lccn.loc.gov/2016003907

Cherry Lake Publishing would like to acknowledge the work of the Partnership for 21st Century Learning. Please visit *www.p21.org* for more information.

Printed in the United States of America
Corporate Graphics

ABOUT THE AUTHOR

Wil Mara is an award-winning and best-selling author of more than 150 books, many of which are educational titles for young readers. Further information about his work can be found at www.wilmara.com.

TABLE OF CONTENTS

CHAPTER 1
Government in the United States 4

CHAPTER 2
How Local Governments Work 10

CHAPTER 3
What It Takes to Do the Job 16

CHAPTER 4
A City Council in Action 22

THINK ABOUT IT 30
FOR MORE INFORMATION 31
GLOSSARY 32
INDEX 32

Government in the United States

Citizens of the United States have certain rights and privileges that are protected by government bodies at three different levels: federal, state, and local. The federal government is the biggest and most powerful. It resides and operates primarily out of our nation's capital, Washington, D.C., and creates laws and maintains services that impact the country as a whole. For example, the federal government is charged with protecting America's borders and fending off foreign invaders. It makes treaties with other governments in hopes of maintaining peaceful and productive relations around the world. "Uncle Sam" does a whole slew of other things, too, including printing money, collecting taxes, running the national parks, and providing social services.

Congress meets in the United States Capitol.

Drivers apply for licenses through their states.

Each state sets its own speed limits.

You are also a resident of one of the 50 states and have to follow the laws that your state government creates. You might live in a state with a big population, like California, or in a state with relatively few people, such as New Mexico or Montana. State governments do not have all the same powers as the federal government. A state can't declare war on a foreign nation or print money, for example. But it does have other, unique responsibilities. It issues licenses for activities such as driving, hunting, and operating a business. A state also decides everyday laws such as the speed limits on major roadways. State

Cities and towns each organize their own garbage collection.

governments also administer federal programs, such as food stamps and housing for low-income families.

Lastly, you are also a resident of a town or city. This is the level at which your **local government** operates. Cities and towns, plus the counties within which they're **incorporated**, have their own powers and responsibilities. These local governments are concerned with the majority of the issues and problems you face on a daily basis. For example, they are responsible for making sure that the garbage is collected, clean water flows into your home, and police are on patrol to keep you safe from crime.

There are certain responsibilities that overlap each level of government. For example, taxes are collected on all three levels. A state government will maintain certain roads, while a local government will maintain others. And law enforcement exists at multiple levels, from the county sheriff to the police to the FBI.

As a citizen, you have two main responsibilities: pay your taxes and obey the laws. You also have another really good responsibility—to speak your mind and, in turn, take part in the governing process. It's not easy for one person to affect policies on the federal level or to change things on the state level, either. But one person can certainly have a powerful effect on a local government's procedures. It gives credibility to the popular phrase, "All politics is local." And local government will likely have the greatest impact on you as you go about your daily life.

How Local Governments Work

The head of a local government is usually a **mayor**, who was elected by the voters, or a city manager hired by the **city council**. City council members are themselves elected by the residents of the city they serve. Large cities may be divided into smaller sections (districts or wards, for example), with a council member representing each.

A local council meets on a regular schedule to take care of the town's business, and these meetings are usually open to the public. Council members vote on issues such as the annual **budget**. During the course of a budgetary discussion, the council might consider applications from people who want to do business with the city, such as builders or maintenance firms. The council will review **zoning** appeals from people who

During council meetings, members often take turns speaking.

Politicians need to be able to explain why they believe in what they do, and how this will affect the people they govern.

want to open a business in one neighborhood or who want to stop a new business from opening in another neighborhood. There are departments within a local government that handle everyday functions such as fire, police, and sanitation services. Larger cities often have many other departments as well, such as planning and development, tourism, and human services.

21st Century Content

Part of being a ***politician*** *in the United States (or really anywhere) means being good at choosing a certain point of view on an issue and then sticking to it. And in the world of politics, that means being challenged from time to time by people—including other politicians—who disagree with you. Politicians spend a lot of time debating their position on these issues, which means they have to believe strongly in them. Think about the things you feel strongly about. How far would you go to defend your beliefs? How sure are you that your beliefs are the right ones?*

Some local governments have teams just to deal with graffiti.

A citizen who has an issue that concerns the local government will contact the department that handles that particular issue. For example, someone who suspects increased gang activity in the neighborhood can ask the police department to increase patrols in that area. Chicago's Department of Streets and Sanitation launched a program called Graffiti Blasters to handle the increasing problem of graffiti on public structures. When new graffiti appeared somewhere, residents called to report it, and a team arrived within two or three days to remove it. As this program proved effective, "taggers" got discouraged when their drawings disappeared so quickly. In turn, graffiti in Chicago began to decrease significantly. This is an excellent example of how a local government can work together with the people it represents to greatly reduce a problem. And it's proof that it's always worthwhile to speak up when something isn't quite right in your neighborhood.

What It Takes to Do the Job

Being a city council member is a fairly demanding job. It means that person has power over the thousands who live in a certain community. So that power should be regarded with the utmost respect and sense of responsibility by the person who holds it. In some larger cities, a council position is a full-time occupation because there are so many people to represent. It pays fairly well for the same reason. In smaller towns, however, council members often receive only a token payment for their services. They often have a day job, as their council duties only require a few hours each week.

So what does it take to be a council member? Towns may require that he or she be a registered voter who has lived in the city for a certain length of time. To be a voter means that the

In smaller towns, being a city council member is only a part-time job.

Sometimes city council candidates need a petition before they can run for office.

candidate for office must be at least 18 years old. Some places require candidates to be 21. Candidates may need to put together a **petition** with the signatures of a certain number of citizens who want them to be council members.

Running a campaign to get elected to local office takes time and money. The campaign process is not easy by any means. The job requires a certain set of skills, talents, and traits, both personal and professional. If political candidates don't have what it takes, then they're not going to get very far.

Running a campaign takes strong people skills.

People go to polling places to cast their votes.

A good candidate has a passion for helping others, because voters are counting on that person to improve their lives. Thus, the best candidates have a great deal of heart and commitment. Other traits include strong organizational skills, a willingness to work hard, tireless determination, and a positive attitude. This last one is much more important than you might think. The candidate needs to stay upbeat when things go wrong—and in the world of politics, they most definitely will!

21st Century Content

How does the voting process work? It's actually pretty simple. Generally speaking, voters go to their local ***polling place*** *in order to cast their vote. This will usually be a public building, such as a school, where voting machines are provided. A typical voting machine is a kind of booth with a curtain acting as the door. Voters step into the booth, and the curtain closes around them. They slide their* ***ballots*** *into the machines. To cast their vote, they might pull small levers by the candidates' names. Or they might have to fill in circles or punch a hole next to their names. Voting machines differ. When done, voters remove the ballot, leave the booth, and place the ballot in a box. More modern voting machines are computerized with touch screens. Some towns prefer to use older machines because computerized systems can be altered, giving false results. And there are still places in America where people simply write down their choices on ballots and slip them into ballot boxes.*

A City Council in Action

Let's look at a city council in the town of Austin, Iowa, to find out how things work in real life. The council held two meetings in April 2007. The first one began typically enough. Minutes from the previous meeting were read and approved. Old business matters were discussed, some of which were resolved, while others warranted further investigation. Then it was time to consider new issues.

Sitting in the audience was a town resident named Noah Lucas. He was concerned about a dangerous intersection in his neighborhood. Lucas had asked Councilwoman Milligan to sponsor a motion to install stop signs at the intersection in an effort to control the flow of traffic and thus make the intersection safer. Milligan investigated the intersection herself. Aside from driving

Traffic issues are one thing addressed in city council meetings.

through it a few times, she took pictures of the daily flow of traffic, and she wrote down the names of local businesses and the locations of nearby playgrounds. When she asked local residents for their opinion, the majority were in favor of adding the stop signs.

Councilman Krouse also gave his opinion. “I was almost run over at that very intersection,” he said. He believed the volume of traffic had significantly increased after a nearby subdivision was built, which led to his close call. He too was in favor of the new stop signs. A third councilman, however, suggested that a more in-depth study be undertaken in order to measure the volume of

Adding stop signs to the right places can make roads safer.

The city council members listened and thought about the issue before voting.

vehicles and pedestrians at the corner.

Mayor Brayman asked if money was available to put up the stop signs immediately, and the town's director of finance said it was. Brayman then suggested skipping the suggested traffic study in order to ensure that the intersection be made safe as quickly as possible. Further discussion followed, and then Brayman called for a vote. The motion was passed, and the mayor said his office would begin the process for installing the stop signs the next day.

Then Councilman Caton presented a petition submitted by store owners near the town's train station. The petition stated that

Politicians need to be able to explain how they can put their ideas into action.

commuters were parking their cars for free in front of the stores instead of paying for parking in the train station's lot like they were supposed to. The owners of these downtown stores were becoming deeply worried. The cars were parked in front of their stores all day, so many townspeople who wanted to shop there had no place to park—and they were doing their shopping instead at the mall outside of town.

Caton's solution to the problem was to install parking meters in front of the stores. That, he said, would encourage commuters to go back to using the station's parking lot and thus free up the spaces in front of the stores. A motion was made to study the idea of installing the parking meters. This motion was approved.

Brayman requested that various council members and city administrators look into different parts of the issue. Caton, for example, would meet with the store owners to determine how many parking meters should be installed. The director of finance would look into the costs of the meters in order to determine the best price for the town, plus how long the installation would take. Brayman said he would speak to the mayor of nearby Bedford Falls to see if the recent installation of parking meters in that town was helping their downtown businesses.

Later, at the second meeting, the parking meters were brought

21st Century Content

Leadership is a quality found in many of America's greatest politicians. In short, leadership is the ability of one person to get others to follow them. For example, in a time of crisis, a good president will inspire the belief that he or she will know how to handle the situation. What specific characteristics do you think a person needs to have in order to be a good leader? Which of those characteristics do you believe you possess?

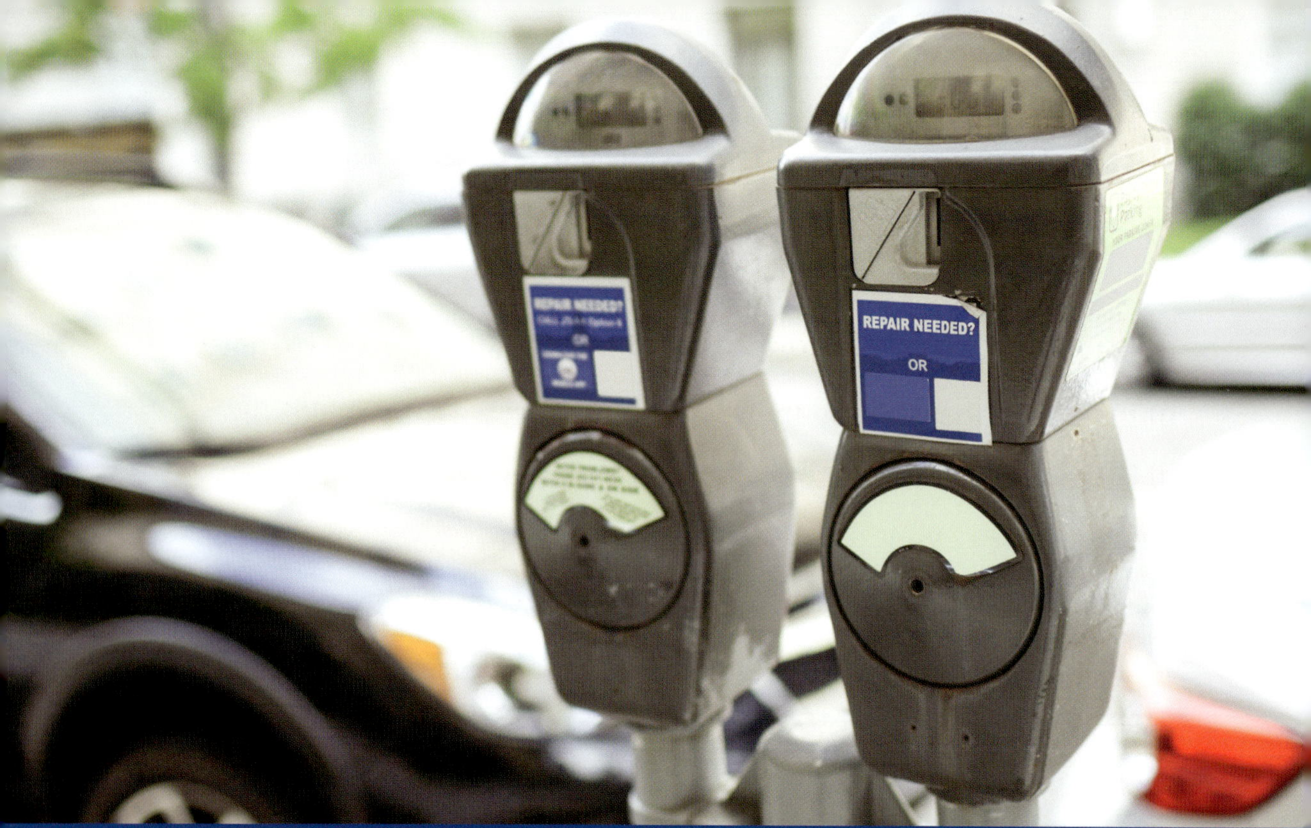

Parking meters help bring in money to the city.

up for discussion. Caton reported that about 280 meters would be needed to protect all the stores near the train station. The director of finance said that installing more than 200 meters would put a heavy financial strain on the city budget. That fact did not go over well with anyone present.

Then Brayman explained what he learned about the situation in Bedford Falls. The new parking meters in that town were generating enough revenue to help pay for the cost of installing them. Further, the businesses there were making more money because the parking spaces were now available to their customers.

As an added bonus, the town of Bedford Falls was taking in more money from the sales taxes that customers paid while shopping in those stores. The mayor of Bedford Falls projected that the parking meters would pay for themselves in about three years!

With their sights firmly set on the long-term benefits rather than the short-term costs, council members voted to install 280 parking meters in downtown Austin. In no time at all, they achieved the desired effect. Local commuters began to park their cars in the train station lot again (where all-day parking was available at a reasonable rate). Local stores began to see their revenues rise again. And the town was getting extra money from the taxes paid by the stores, the parking meters themselves, and the fees from the train's parking lot.

The store owners were people who saw problems in their community and brought them to their local government for discussion. And the local leaders worked to come up with effective solutions. This interaction between ordinary citizens and their local government is an outstanding example of the true value of American **democracy**.

Think About It

Check your local newspaper. What's one issue your city council has addressed lately? What did they do about it? Do you agree with how they handled it?

Imagine you are running for city council. Why should people vote for you? What skills could you bring to the government? Which important issues would you address?

Some city council meetings are open for the public to attend. Check your local newspaper and try to go to one soon. Write a paragraph about the experience. Or, if you can't go, write a paragraph about what you imagine it would be like.

For More Information

BOOKS

Goodman, Susan E., and Elwood Smith (illustrator). *See How They Run: Campaign Dreams, Election Schemes, and the Race to the White House.* New York: Bloomsbury, 2012.

Krull, Kathleen, and Anna DiVito (illustrator). *A Kid's Guide to America's Bill of Rights.* New York: HarperCollins, 2015.

Winter, Jonah, and Barry Blitt (illustrator). *The Founding Fathers! The Horse-Ridin', Fiddle-Playin', Book-Readin', Gun-Totin' Gentlemen Who Started America.* New York: Atheneum, 2015.

ON THE WEB

Congress for Kids—Elections: Political Parties
www.congressforkids.net/Elections_politicalparties.htm

Kids.gov—Government
https://kids.usa.gov/government/index.shtml

PBS Kids—The Democracy Project: How Does Government Affect Me?
http://pbskids.org/democracy/my-government/

GLOSSARY

ballots (BAL-uhtz) a way of voting secretly, using a machine or slips of paper

budget (BUHJ-it) a plan for how much money you will earn and spend during a particular period of time

candidate (KAN-di-date) a person who is running for office in an election

city council (SIT-ee KOUN-suhl) a group of people chosen to run a city

democracy (dih-MAH-kruh-see) a form of government in which the people choose their leaders in elections

incorporated (in-KOR-puh-ray-tid) included as part of a city or county

local government (LOH-kuhl GUHV-urn-muhnt) the group of people who govern the town or city in which you live

mayor (MAY-ur) a person who is elected to be the leader of a town or city government

petition (puh-TISH-uhn) a letter signed by many people telling those in power they want something done

politician (pah-lih-TISH-uhn) a person who runs for or holds a government office

polling place (POHL-ing place) the place where votes are cast and recorded during an election

zoning (ZOHN-ing) sections in a city or town that have been set up to have different purposes

INDEX

budgets, 10, 13, 32

campaigns, 18–20
candidates, 18, 20–21
city managers, 10
council meetings, 10–13
  how they work, 22–29
  members, 16–21

federal government, 4, 7, 9

government, 4–9
graffiti, 14, 15

laws, 4, 7, 9
licenses, 6, 7
local government, 6, 8–9
  departments, 13, 15
  how it works, 10–15

mayor, 10, 25, 27, 29

parking issues, 26–29
petitions, 18, 25–26
politicians, 12, 13, 27

state government, 4, 6, 7–9

taxes, 4, 9
traffic issues, 7, 22–25

voting, 16, 18, 20, 21